BACKYARD COOKBOOK

Rob Rees

Crabtree Publishing Company
www.crabtreebooks.com

Author: Rob Rees
Editor: Crystal Sikkens
Project coordinator: Kathy Middleton
Production coordinator: Ken Wright
Prepress technician: Margaret Amy Salter
Series consultant: Gill Matthews

Picture Credits:
Dreamstime: (Cover) Ireneusz Sinicki, Claudio Baldini 4b, 20tr, Susabell 15
Istockphoto: Piotr Antonów 18tr, 19, Toby Creamer 13b (main), Floortje 7, Marek Pawluczuk 6tl, Peter Seager 6tr
Shutterstock: Cover, Titov Andriy 14tl, Andrjuss 10tl, Norman Chan 16tl, Elli 9, S. Fierros 10tr, Douglas Freer 14tr, Magdalena Kucova 8tr, Robyn Mackenzie 17, Monkey Business Images 11, 21, Newo 20tl, Ostromec 12tr, Marek Pawluczuk 16tr, Vishal Shah 4t, 8tl, Rui Vale de Sousa 18tl, Bartosz Wardzinski 13b (inset), Dusan Zidar 12tl
Illustration: Istockphoto: Ronnie Sampson.

Library and Archives Canada Cataloguing in Publication

Rees, Rob, 1968-
     Backyard cookbook / Rob Rees.

(Crabtree connections)
Includes index.
ISBN 978-0-7787-9939-9 (bound).--ISBN 978-0-7787-9961-0 (pbk.)

     1. Cookery--Juvenile literature. 2. Seasonal cookery--Juvenile literature. 3. Gardening--Juvenile literature. I. Title.
II. Series: Crabtree connections.

TX652.5.R43 2010   j641.5'123   C2010-901506-1

Library of Congress Cataloging-in-Publication Data

Rees, Rob, 1968-
     Backyard cookbook / Rob Rees.
        p. cm. -- (Crabtree connections)
     Includes index.
ISBN 978-0-7787-9961-0 (pbk. : alk. paper) - ISBN 978-0-7787-9939-9 (reinforced library binding : alk. paper)
1. Cookery--Juvenile literature. 2. Gardening--Juvenile literature. I. Title. II. Series.

TX652.5.R44 2011
641.5--dc22
                                               2010008050

Crabtree Publishing Company

Printed in the U.S.A./062010/WO20100815

Published in Canada
Crabtree Publishing
616 Welland Ave.
St. Catharines, Ontario
L2M 5V6

Published in the United States
Crabtree Publishing
PMB 59051
350 Fifth Avenue, 59th Floor
New York, New York 10118

Contents

Food is Fun

Cooking and growing food can be a lot of fun. Sharing a meal with friends and family is also a good way to spend time together. Inside this book you will find a lot of fun recipes to make great dishes.

Cooking with the seasons

You can see different fruits and vegetables in the garden at different times of the year. We call these divisions in the year the seasons.

The recipes in this book use some of the fruits or vegetables from each of the four seasons: Spring, summer, fall, and winter. Simply follow the instructions on each page.

Beets can be grown in the fall.

Peas can be grown in the summer.

Some recipes need more attention or more time to make.

How to use your ingredients

Tips straight from the chef

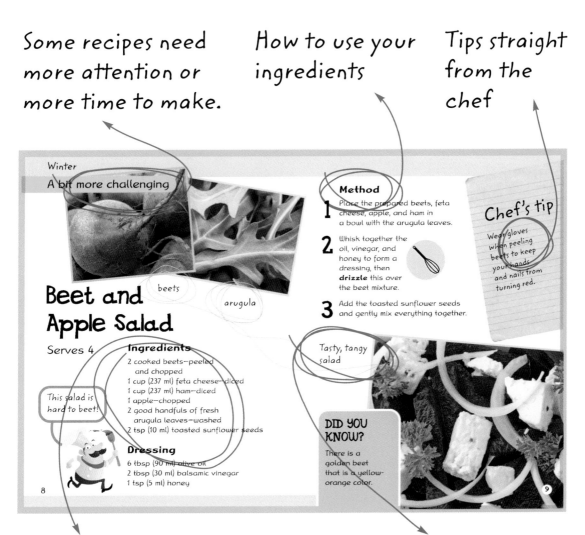

Winter

A bit more challenging

Beet and Apple Salad

Serves 4

beets

arugula

This salad is hard to beet!

Ingredients

2 cooked beets—peeled and chopped
1 cup (237 ml) feta cheese—diced
1 cup (237 ml) ham—diced
1 apple—chopped
2 good handfuls of fresh arugula leaves—washed
2 tsp (10 ml) toasted sunflower seeds

Dressing

6 tbsp (90 ml) olive oil
2 tbsp (30 ml) balsamic vinegar
1 tsp (5 ml) honey

8

Method

1 Place the prepared beets, feta cheese, apple, and ham in a bowl with the arugula leaves.

2 Whisk together the oil, vinegar, and honey to form a dressing, then **drizzle** this over the beet mixture.

3 Add the toasted sunflower seeds and gently mix everything together.

Chef's tip

Wear gloves when peeling beets to keep your hands and nails from turning red.

Tasty, tangy salad

DID YOU KNOW?

There is a golden beet that is a yellow-orange color.

9

Everything you will need to make the recipe

The finished product!

REMEMBER!

Always ask an adult for help before using the kitchen to make these recipes.

leeks

potatoes

Leek and Potato Soup

Serves 4

Ingredients

2 large leeks—
  washed and sliced
2 tbsp (30 ml) butter
2 medium potatoes—peeled,
  washed, and diced
2½ cups (592 ml) vegetable stock
1¼ cups (296 ml) milk
Freshly ground black pepper
Grated nutmeg

Serve with crusty bread.

Method

1 Fry the leeks gently in the butter for 3 minutes. Stir frequently.

2 Add the potatoes and cook gently for another 2 minutes.

3 Add the milk and stock and bring to a boil.

4 Reduce the heat and **simmer** until the potatoes are cooked (about 25 minutes).

5 Mix in a blender or with a hand blender.

6 **Season** with pepper and grated nutmeg.

Ta da! Delicious soup

Chef's tip

Chop off the **frayed** green ends of your leeks. They are too **bitter** to eat.

DID YOU KNOW?

Leeks are packed full of vitamins that help fight colds.

A bit more challenging

Beet and Apple Salad

beets

arugula

Serves 4

Ingredients

2 cooked beets—peeled
  and chopped
1 cup (237 ml) feta cheese—diced
1 cup (237 ml) ham—diced
1 apple—chopped
2 good handfuls of fresh
  arugula leaves—washed
2 tsp (10 ml) toasted sunflower seeds

Dressing

6 tbsp (90 ml) olive oil
2 tbsp (30 ml) balsamic vinegar
1 tsp (5 ml) honey

This salad is
hard to beet!

Method

1 Place the prepared beets, feta cheese, apple, and ham in a bowl with the arugula leaves.

2 Whisk together the oil, vinegar, and honey to form a dressing, then **drizzle** this over the beet mixture.

3 Add the toasted sunflower seeds and gently mix everything together.

Chef's tip

Wear gloves when peeling beets to keep your hands and nails from turning red.

Tasty, tangy salad

DID YOU KNOW?

There is a golden beet that is a yellow-orange color.

A bit more challenging

ginger

rhubarb

Crunchy Sweet 'n' Sour Bake

Serves 4

Ingredients

4 cups (948 ml) rhubarb
3 tbsp (45 ml) water
$\frac{1}{2}$ cup (118 ml) white sugar
1 cup (237 ml) flour
$\frac{1}{2}$ cup (118 ml) butter
$\frac{2}{3}$ cup (158 ml) brown sugar
1 tsp (5 ml) ground ginger

Serve with custard or ice cream.

Method

1 Preheat oven to 400°F (204°C)

2 Wash the rhubarb then cut diagonally.

3 Place in a saucepan with the water and white sugar. Cook gently until the rhubarb begins to soften.

4 Place the mixture in an **ovenproof** dish.

5 Put the remaining ingredients in a bowl. Rub between your fingers to make crumbs.

6 Sprinkle the crumbs over the rhubarb to cover it.

7 Place in the oven for 20 minutes until golden and crisp.

Mouthwatering rhubarb and ice cream

DID YOU KNOW?

Pulling rhubarb out of the ground keeps it fresher than cutting it.

asparagus

avocado

Asparagus and Guacamole Dip

Serves 4

Ingredients

1 bunch of asparagus—washed
4 handfuls of mixed salad
   leaves, to garnish
2 ripe avocados
4 fresh tomatoes
Juice of half a lemon
1 tsp (5 ml) ground black pepper

Get dipping!

Method
To make the dip

1 Cut each avocado in half lengthways. Carefully remove the pit.

2 Scoop out the insides into a bowl. Mash into a smooth paste with a fork.

3 Mix in the lemon juice and pepper.

4 Dice the tomatoes roughly and stir them into the creamy mixture.

To cook the asparagus

1 Remove the bottom inch from the asparagus.

2 Cook the asparagus in boiling water for 2 minutes.

3 Drain the asparagus through a **colander**.

4 Serve warm or cold.

Yummy asparagus and guacamole dip

DID YOU KNOW?

Asparagus is a **relative** of the lily flower.

Easy

Fruit Smoothie

raspberries

bananas

Serves 4

Ingredients

$2/3$ cup (158 ml) fresh strawberries
$2/3$ cup (158 ml) fresh raspberries
1 ripe banana, sliced
1 cup (237 ml) plain low-fat yogurt
$1 1/4$ cups (296 ml) milk
6 to 8 ice cubes

Experiment with other fruits
and flavored yogurts.

Method

1 Wash the berries.

2 Place fruit, yogurt, and milk into a blender or food processor and **purée** until smooth. Add a little extra milk if you want it to be thinner.

3 Add the ice cubes and blend again for another 20 to 30 seconds until the ice is roughly crushed. Serve immediately.

Really fruity fruit smoothie

Chef's tip

Raspberries can **spoil** quickly. It is best to keep them in the fridge until you are ready to use them. Wash them just before using.

DID YOU KNOW?

Fruit smoothies are packed with the **vitamins** that keep your body in great shape.

strawberries

lemon

Strawberry Zinger

Serves 4

Ingredients

1 basket of strawberries
1 lemon
4 slices of sushi ginger
(available from most grocery stores)
2 level tsp (10 ml) confectioner's or
icing sugar

Serve in a bowl
with cream and
shortbread cookies.

Method

1 Wash strawberries and remove the green tops.

2 Cut strawberries into four pieces and put in a bowl.

3 Finely chop ginger and add to the bowl.

4 Grate half the lemon peel and add to the bowl.

5 Squeeze the juice from the lemon and add to the bowl.

6 Sift the confectioner's sugar into the bowl.

7 Mix the strawberries around a couple of times—be gentle though!

8 Leave them for 10 minutes before serving.

Sugary-sweet strawberries

DID YOU KNOW?

27,000 strawberries and 1,876 gallons (7,098 liters) of cream were eaten at the Wimbledon Tennis Championships in the U.K. in 2007.

A bit more challenging

pears

mint

Sticky Toffee Pears

Serves 4

Ingredients

4 pears—washed
1/4 cup (59 ml) butter
1/2 cup (118 ml) brown sugar
1 cup (237 ml) whipping cream
Piece of mint—roughly chopped

Pears are also delicious in salads with a **vinaigrette** dressing.

Method

1 Cut the pears into four pieces and remove the core.

2 Melt the butter in a frying pan.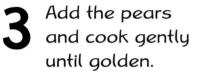

3 Add the pears and cook gently until golden.

4 Stir in the sugar gently, while turning the fruit.

5 When the sugar starts to melt, add the cream.

6 Bring to a boil and keep boiling until the cream is thick.

7 Remove from heat and add the chopped mint. Serve with a scoop of vanilla ice cream.

Mouthwatering pears and ice cream

DID YOU KNOW?

In 1640 there were only 60 types of pears. Today there are over 3,500 types.

Mushy Peas

mint

peas

Serves 4

Ingredients

3 cups (711 ml) fresh peas
¼ cup (59 ml) mashed potatoes
  (still warm)
2 tbsp (30 ml) butter
1 tsp (5 ml) chopped fresh mint
Pinch cracked black pepper
Some milk (if needed)

Mushy peas taste great with fish!

Method

1 Place the peas in a saucepan. Add enough boiling water to just cover them. Cook for 2 minutes.

2 Drain the water using a colander. Add the mashed potatoes to the peas.

3 Stir in the butter and mash everything together. Add a drop of milk if it looks a bit dry.

4 Stir in the mint and cracked black pepper just before serving.

Chef's tip

Steam peas to keep in their vitamins and goodness. You can steam peas in an electric steamer, in the microwave, or in a steamer over a pan of boiling water.

Minty and mushy peas

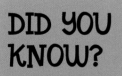

DID YOU KNOW?

The world record for eating peas with chopsticks is 7,175 peas in 1 hour.

21

Glossary

bitter Tastes very sharp and not sweet

colander Container with holes. When a mixture is placed inside a colander, the liquid is drained from it, but the solid material is left behind

drizzle To cover very lightly

frayed Ragged and torn

grated Shredded, using a metal grater

ovenproof Dish that can be placed in a hot oven

purée To mash or blend something until it is smooth

relative Belonging to the same family group

season To improve the flavor by adding herbs or spices

simmer To cook on a very low heat

spoil To go bad or start to rot

vinaigrette Salad dressing made from oil, vinegar, and seasoning

vitamins Goodness in food that keeps bodies healthy

Further Information

Web sites

Find out more about food and healthy eating at:
www.greatgrubclub.com

Discover how to cook and eat healthy at:
www.spatulatta.com

Enter your own healthy recipes and see if you can win the cooking competition at:
www.kids-cooking-activities.com/cooking-recipe-contest.html

Books

Mom and Me Cookbook by Annabel Karmel. DK Children (2005).

Green Food Fun by Lisa Bullard. Capstone Press (2006).

Star Cooks—Recipes by Celebrity Chefs. Dorling Kindersley (2006).

Index